Dream & Vision Journal

This book belongs to:

_____

Independently published by Bee Ministries.
Manila, Arkansas

ISBN: 979-8-9887297-2-3

All scriptures used in this journal come from the King James Version of the Bible.

Check out Sheila's other works on Amazon:
Life After the Mistake
How to Bee Prosperous
How to Be Intentional: With Your Words
How to Be Healthy, Wealthy, and Wise
How to Be Prayerful, Powerful, and Purposeful
ebook: *How to Be a Writer*

Find Sheila on YouTube at Bee Ministries
Facebook @LifeAfterTheMistake

Dream & Vision Journal

From Sheila Textor, Bee Ministries

Write Your Vision with Victory!

Introduction

Our imagination is a beautiful gift from God. Everything about God is creative. In the book of Genesis, each time God spoke something into existence, He would see that it was good. We are the children of God. We have His DNA. When we were children, we would play and imagine different roles. Teachers, doctors, nurses, cowboys, and Indians usually were the top ones. As we get older, we realize we can't pretend anymore. Life has a way of pulling you back to reality.

That is why I wanted to create a place for you to dream again. Bring that child-like faith back into your heart. In Psalm 126:1 it says, "When the Lord turned again the captivity of Zion, we were like them that dream."

Go ahead and dream. Go ahead and believe. Let your mind imagine a great future. Whatever that may look like for you.

We are not here promoting name it and claim it, or blab it and grab it. This has nothing to do with trying to get bigger or better than anyone else. This is a place to let the things you feel called to come to fruition.

I will use myself as an example. I have a goal of writing 12 devotionals. I believe someday they will be in bookstores all over the US, even the world. More than making book sales, my heart's desire is to inspire my readers to believe God's Word. I have my own vision-casting book. Pictures of the books being in bookstores. Pictures of me at book signings. Each picture has a scripture and a decree. It's not just about me. My children and grandchildren will be impacted by the work of my hands today.

I want to encourage you today to pray and seek God for His will in your life. Whatever you feel in your spirit, put it in this vision journal. Maybe you feel called to write as well. Cut out a picture of a book or draw a picture, find a scripture that lines up with that call, write it out.

Don't feel confined to write between the lines. Do what your heart feels.

Look at your visions and dreams and goals as often as you can. Meditate on the scripture you used. Reread your why. How will this goal move the kingdom of God forward?

The scripture that we built this vision book on is found in Habakkuk 2:2: "And the LORD answered me, and said, Write the vision, and make it plain upon tables, that he may run that readeth it."

So go on and write your visions, dreams, and goals. The Lord is listening.

-Sheila

My Dreams and Visons
(sample)

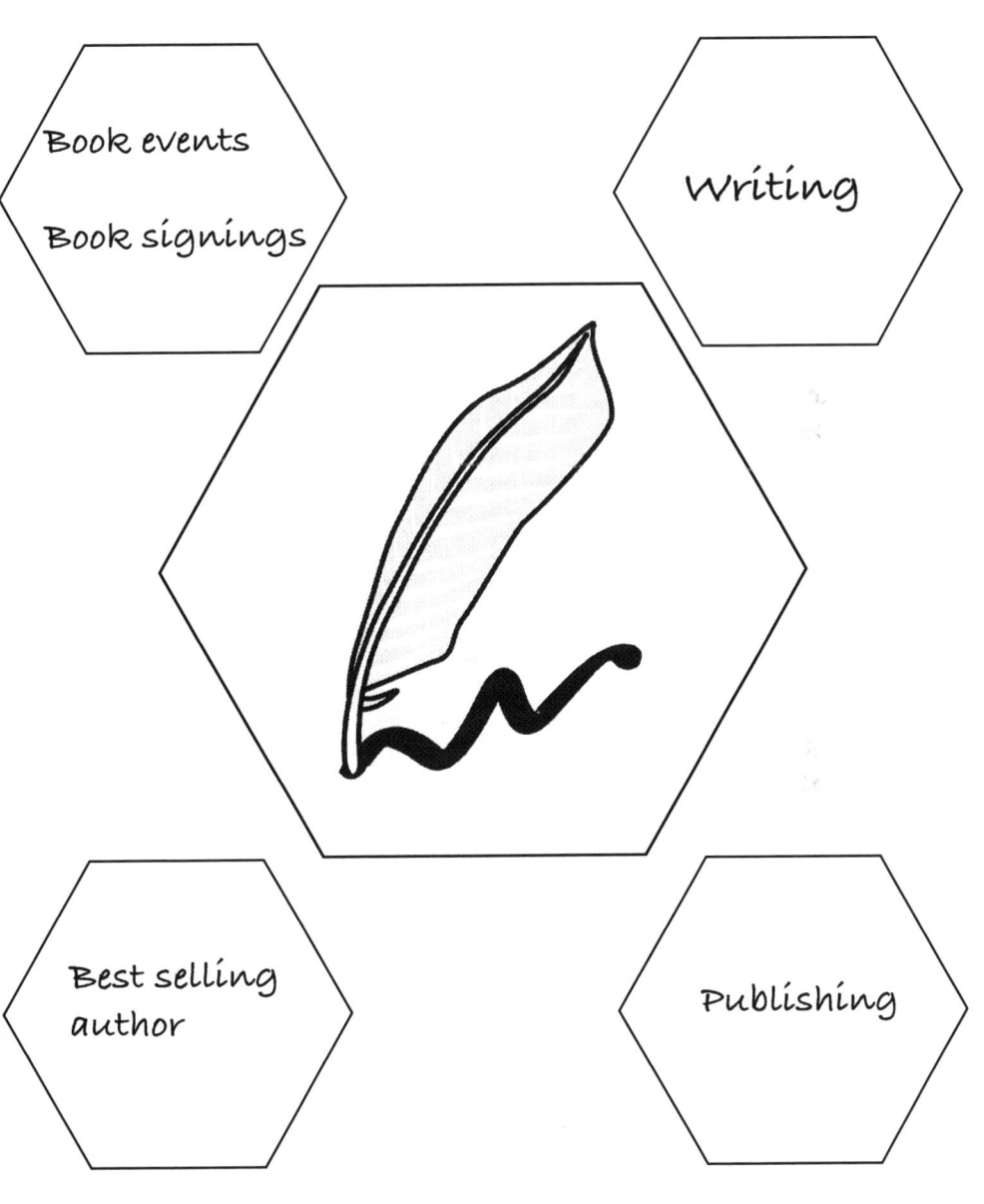

Book events

Book signings

Writing

Best selling author

Publishing

Write it out

Write the vision and make it plain... Habakkuk 2:2

_____

_____

_____

_____

_____

_____

_____

_____

_____

_____

Date completed:
(Come back and write it later!)

Add as much as you want to your honeycombs!

Draw or paste pictures in the box to show your vision

Write it out

Write the vision and make it plain... Habakkuk 2:2

_____

_____

_____

_____

_____

_____

_____

_____

_____

_____

Message from Victory:

You're doing great! What have you done today or this week to work toward your goal?

_____

_____

_____

_____

_____

_____

_____

_____

Draw or paste pictures here

Write it out

Write the vision and make it plain... Habakkuk 2:2

_____

_____

_____

_____

_____

_____

_____

_____

_____

_____

Write it out

Write the vision and make it plain... Habakkuk 2:2

_____

_____

_____

_____

_____

_____

_____

_____

_____

_____

Write it out

Write the vision and make it plain... Habakkuk 2:2

_____

_____

_____

_____

_____

_____

_____

_____

_____

_____

What about your **DREAMS?**

Does anything you feel called toward feel like a pipe dream? Write it out.

Have you had any interesting dreams while sleeping? It could be recently or far in the past.

_____

_____

_____

_____

_____

_____

_____

_____

_____

_____

Draw or paste pictures related to your dream

Write it out

Write the vision and make it plain... Habakkuk 2:2

_____

_____

_____

_____

_____

_____

_____

_____

_____

_____

Draw or paste pictures here

Write it out

Write the vision and make it plain... Habakkuk 2:2

_____

_____

_____

_____

_____

_____

_____

_____

_____

_____

Write it out

Write the vision and make it plain... Habakkuk 2:2

_____

_____

_____

_____

_____

_____

_____

_____

_____

_____

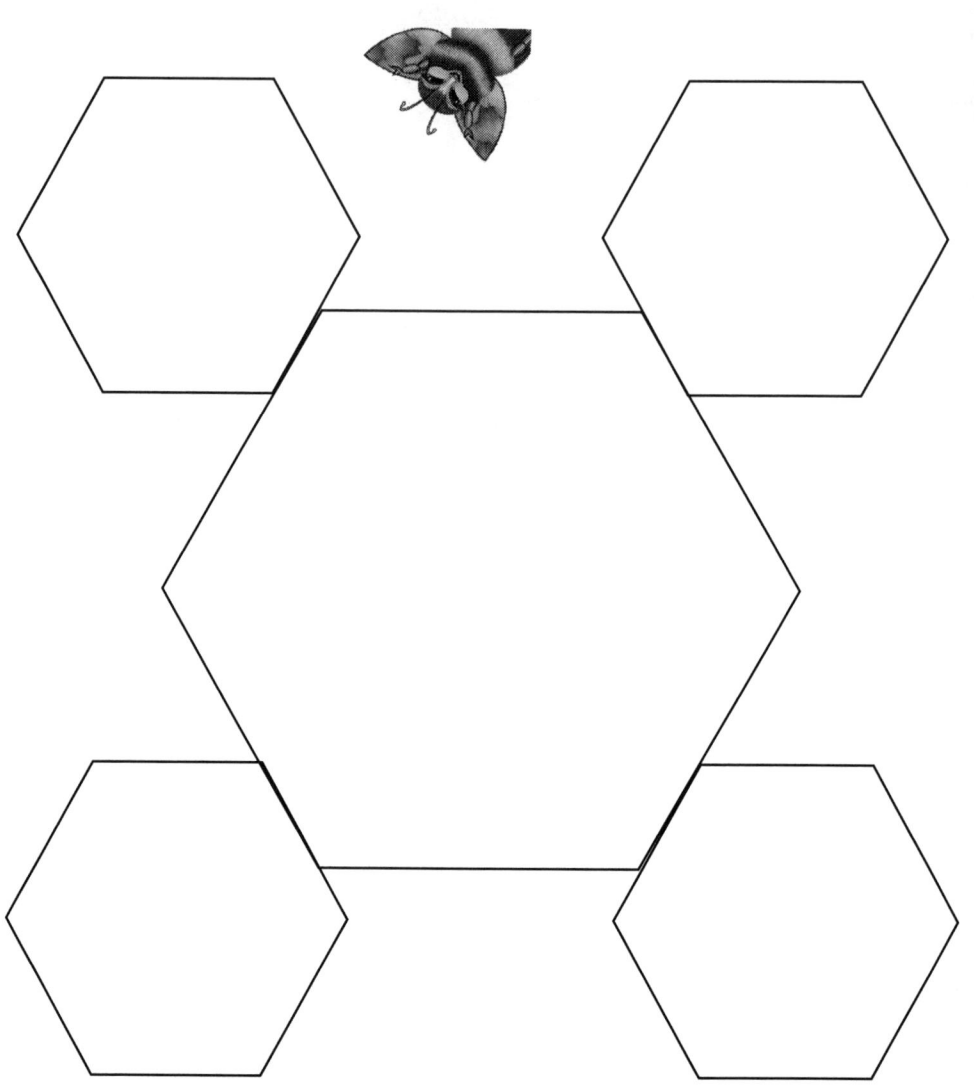

Write it out

Write the vision and make it plain... Habakkuk 2:2

_____

_____

_____

_____

_____

_____

_____

_____

_____

_____

Draw or paste pictures here

Write it out

Write the vision and make it plain... Habakkuk 2:2

_____

_____

_____

_____

_____

_____

_____

_____

_____

_____

Are you experiencing **VICTORY?**

Take a moment now to write out some thanksgivings to the Lord. Even if things aren't going well, what can you be thankful for today?

_____

_____

_____

_____

_____

_____

_____

_____

_____

_____

_____

_____

Write it out

Write the vision and make it plain... Habakkuk 2:2

_____

_____

_____

_____

_____

_____

_____

_____

_____

_____

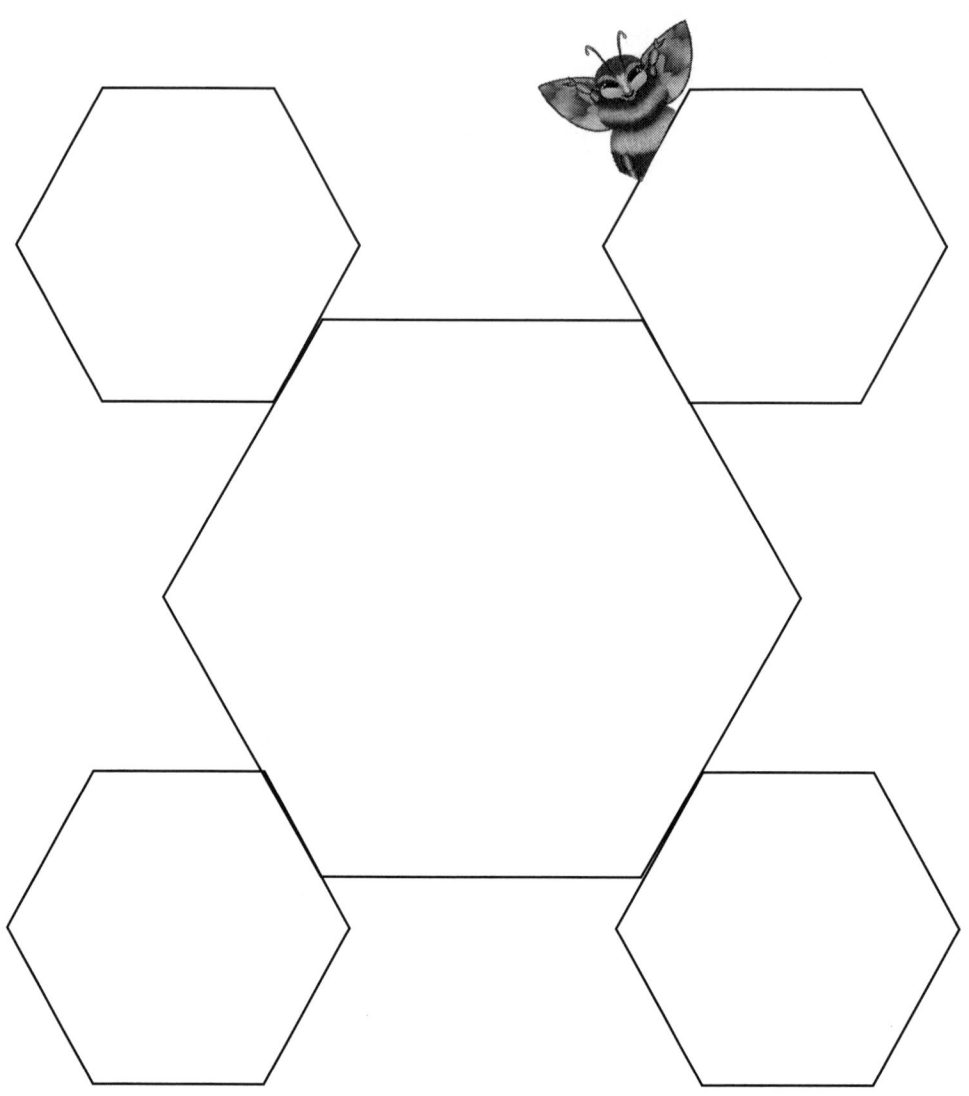

REFLECT
Create a simple list of your dreams, visions, and goals so far.

1. _____

2. _____

3. _____

4. _____

5. _____

6. _____

7. _____

8. _____

9. _____

10. _____

11. _____

12. _____

13. _____

14. _____

15. _____

16. _____

17. _____

PRAYER PAUSE

Take a moment to write a prayer to the Lord about your vision and goals. Include your hangups, setbacks, or steps forward.

_____

_____

_____

_____

_____

_____

_____

_____

_____

Write it out

Write the vision and make it plain... Habakkuk 2:2

Draw or paste pictures in the box to show your vision

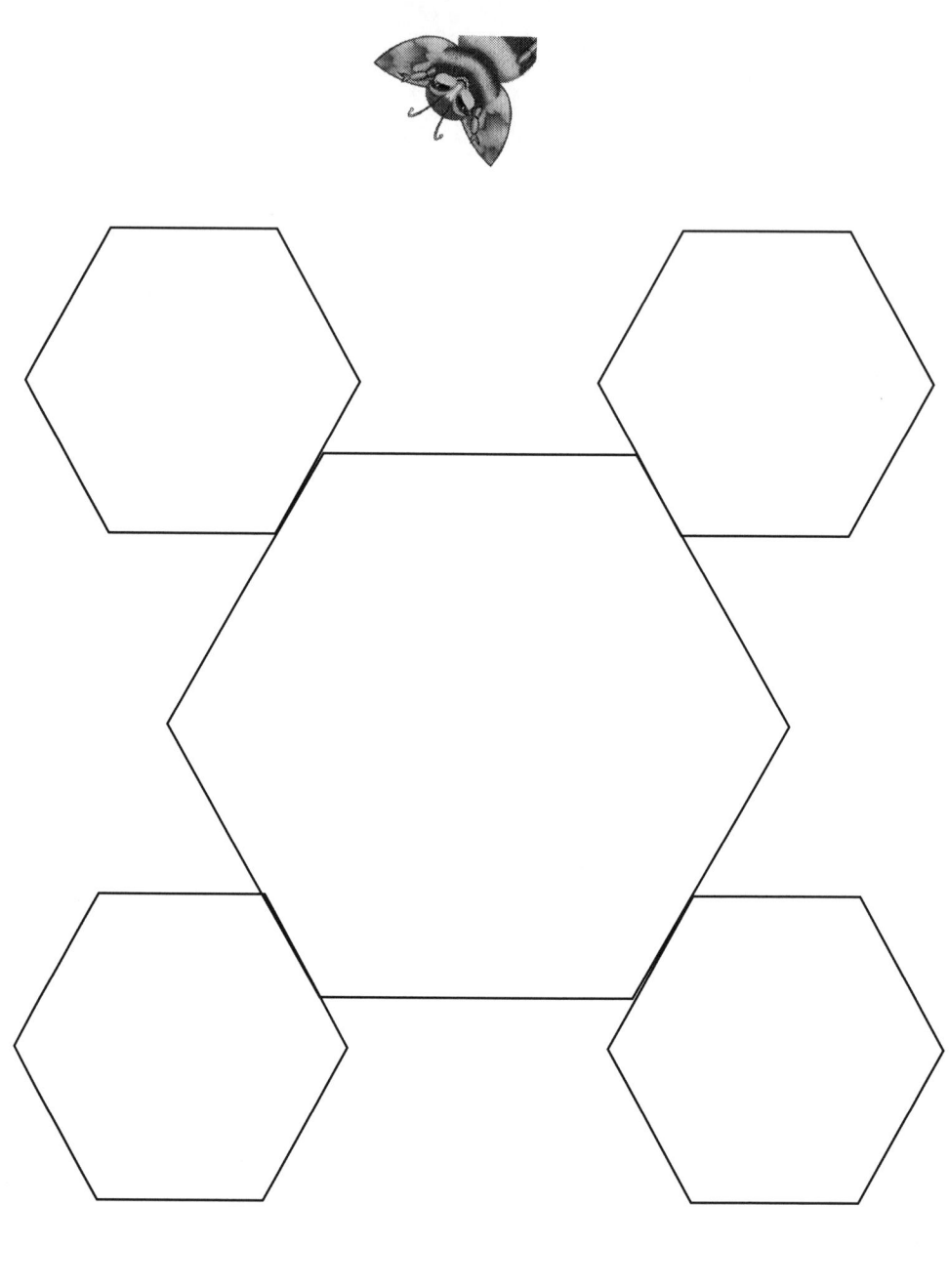

Write it out

Write the vision and make it plain... Habakkuk 2:2

_____

_____

_____

_____

_____

_____

_____

_____

_____

_____

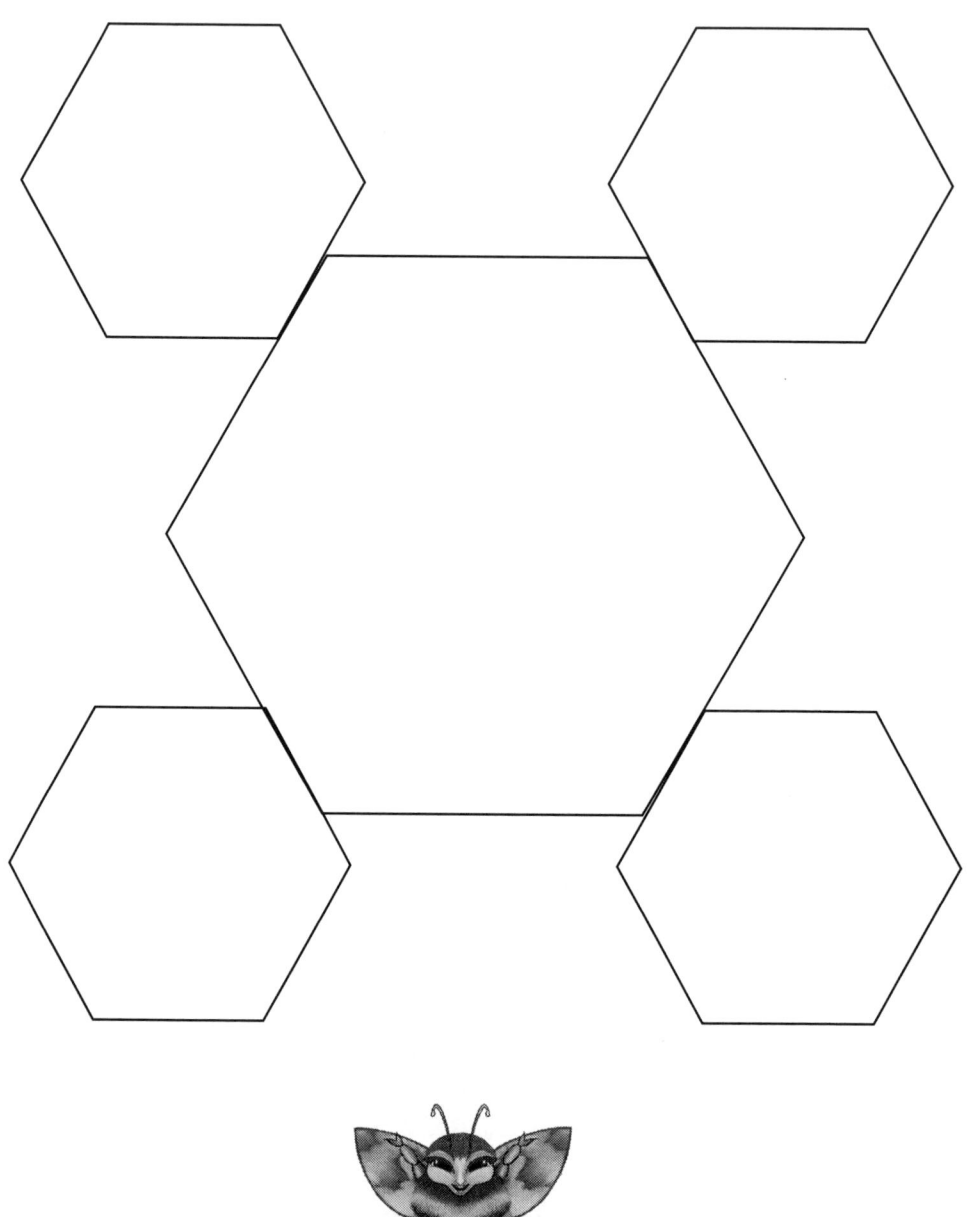

Write it out

Write the vision and make it plain... Habakkuk 2:2

_____

_____

_____

_____

_____

_____

_____

_____

_____

_____

Draw or paste pictures here

WRITE WITH COURAGE

It takes courage to act upon a vision.

What has encouraged you lately?

What are some challenges you face that will take courage to overcome?

And ye are Christ's; and Christ is God's.
1 Corinthians 3:23

_____

_____

_____

_____

_____

_____

_____

_____

_____

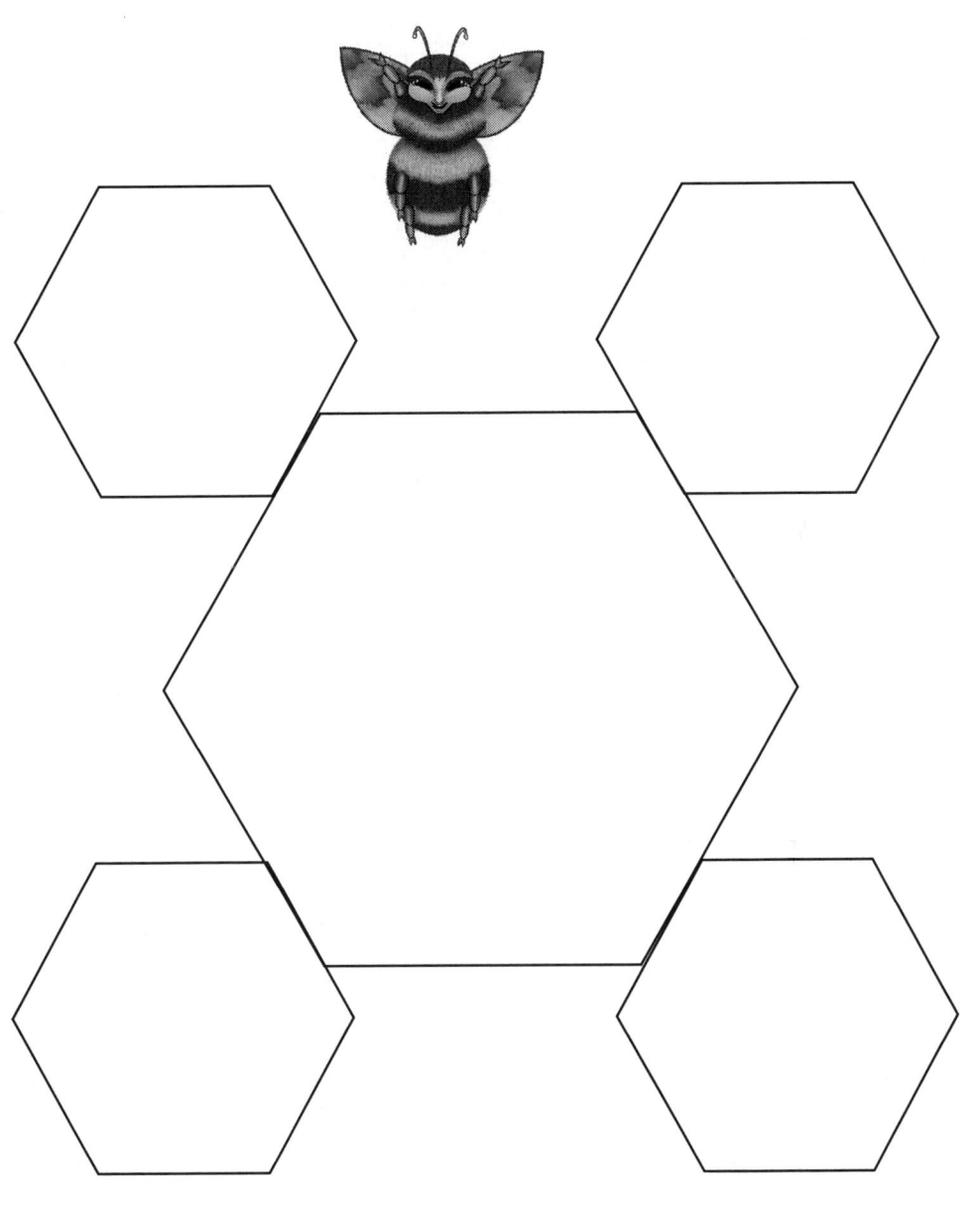

Write it out

Write the vision and make it plain... Habakkuk 2:2

_____

_____

_____

_____

_____

_____

_____

_____

_____

_____

Message from Victory:

Your visions, dreams, goals, and anything you want to do in your life must be placed in the hands of the Lord first. You must also act and work to achieve it.

How is it all going?

Draw or paste pictures here

Write it out

Write the vision and make it plain... Habakkuk 2:2

_____

_____

_____

_____

_____

_____

_____

_____

_____

_____

Draw or paste pictures in the box to show your vision

Write it out

Write the vision and make it plain... Habakkuk 2:2

_____

_____

_____

_____

_____

_____

_____

_____

_____

_____

YOUR JOURNEY CONTINUES

No matter how close you are to achieving your goal now, you have kept that vision close throughout your work in this journal.

What's next for you now?

For which cause we faint not; but though our outward man perish, yet the inward man is renewed day by day.
2 Corinthians 4:16

_____

_____

_____

_____

_____

_____

_____

_____

_____

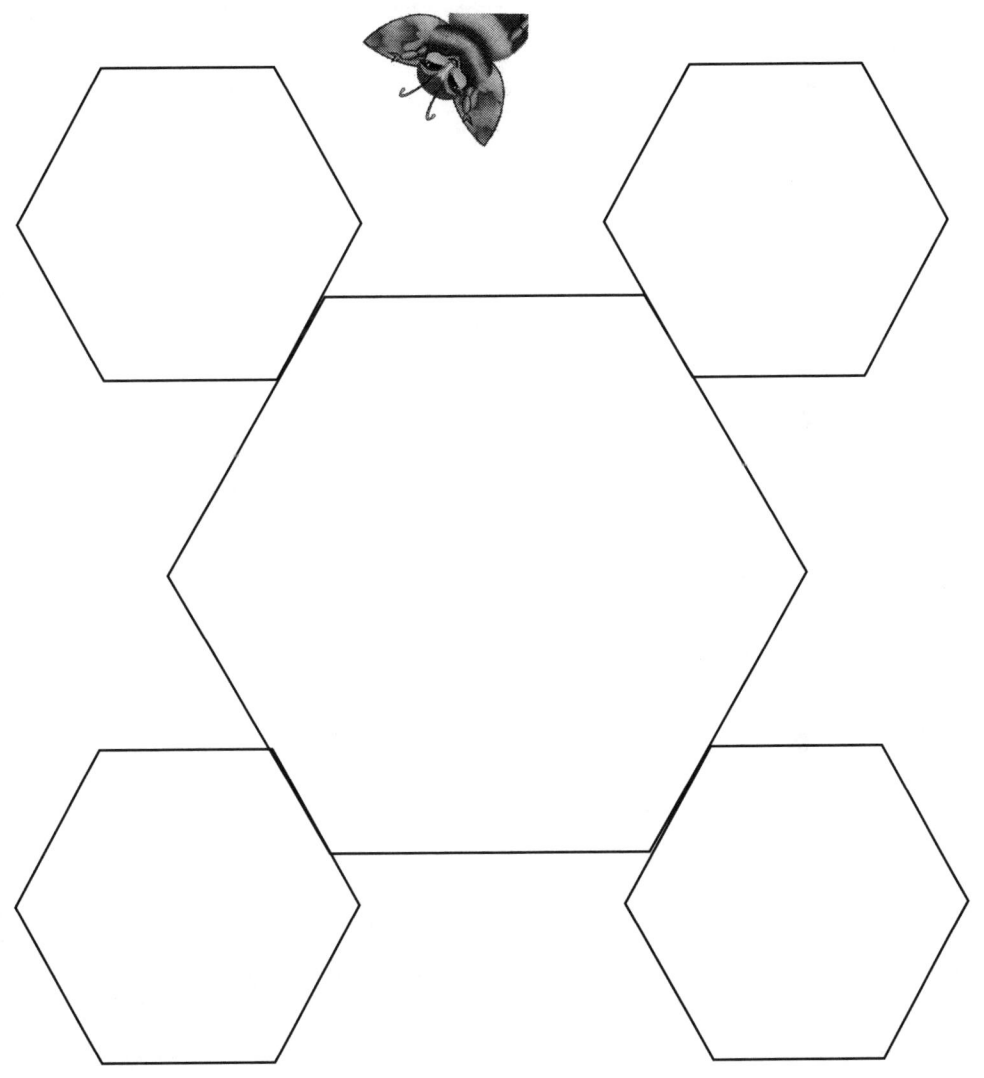

Made in the USA
Middletown, DE
16 November 2025